# Enid and her Two Mums

## Jessica Skogstad

illustrations Tara Reynolds

A special mention to my son, Clark and my niece, Quorra. You are both already leading the way in teaching other kids about what really matters. I love you both with all my heart.

Enid and Her Two Mums

Copyright © Jessica Skogstad
Illustration copyright © Tara Reynolds

First Edition 2016
Published by Aly's Books

www.alysbooks.com
Your Book | Our Mission
Edited by Irrefutable Proof
www.irrefutable-proof.com

Designed by Fish Biscuit
fishbiscuitdesign.com.au

All rights reserved. No part of this book may be reproduced or transmitted in any form or by any means, electronic, mechanical, photocopying or otherwise without the prior permission of the publisher.

ISBN: 9780994401595

Enid walked to school one day...

She noticed so many interesting things along the way.

Across the road, Sally had her mum on her right side.
To her left, her dad followed with pride.

Alex, Marcy, Emmett, Sue,
Esther and Xander, too.
They all walked with their
mums and dads, right on cue.

Enid looked from left to right,
before receiving a big hug, ever so tight!
Enid's two mums held her close,
before farewelling her, "Adios!"

She wondered why she had two mums and no dad,
the other kids had one of each – it made her sad!
Enid spent all day asking, "why, why, why?"
She wanted to understand and promised to try!

After school, she met her mums again. She told them how she'd learnt to count to ten.

She looked around and saw her mates, with their mums and dads, leaving the school gates.

She then decided to look some more.
Surely there were other kids and their
parents she could explore!

Peter jostled up ahead,
his only companion, his father, Fred.

Anouk dawdled way behind.
On her own – she didn't seem to mind.
Rex walked alone as well,
lonely and bored, he didn't look so swell.

Evan raced past them all,
into his mum's arms,
where he looked so small.

Ned and Ted piggybacked
all the way,
to their mum and dad,
waiting in the parking bay.

Then Enid looked around and noticed something quite profound.
Stanley and his two dads walked hand-in-hand, no mummy to be found!

Enid noticed how happy Stanley seemed.
He was chatting to his dads, while Enid just daydreamed!

Enid wondered why she had been so confused.
After all, love from her mums was never refused.

She had two very special parents who loved her like mad. What did it matter if neither of them was a dad?

Peter and Evan weren't so different, too.
Their single parents loved them enough for two!

She realised how lucky she had always been.
To have her two mums was like a dream!

She turned around and ran behind.
Anouk and Rex, she had to find!

She brought them up to meet her mums.
She smiled and smiled, showing teeth and gums.

She explained to her friends, "my mums are special to me, they have enough love for us three!"

She knew now that it didn't matter if she had a mum and a dad, two mums, two dads or just one. All that mattered was that she was loved a tonne.

Enid looked at her mums and smiled.
She said, "I'm so happy I am your child!"

## Acknowledgements

The following wonderful people have each contributed towards getting Enid and Her Two Mums out into the world through their support, donations and presale purchases. For this, I thank them all immensely.

Allisha Ellul
Ann Cauchi
Ash and Rob Findlay
Ava and Eli Broome
Belinda Keay
Brandy, Justin, Isabella and Josh Magro
Brenda Kukucka
Cameron Cook (with Chris and Rosie)
Cathy Filardo
Christopher Skogstad
Danielle Winnacott
Diane, Richard, Naomi, Cassie, Christian and Josh
Ellen Smith
Gabriella Farrugia

Gina Magro
Grace Thiry
Jane Daniels
Joanne Sciberras
John and Sarah Cassar
John and Wendy Sciberras
John Hogg
Karen Carter and Hobsons Bay Family Day Care
Kate Richardson
Katherine Peng
Kathy Myall
Kylie Norris
Lan Pham
Leah Persich
Louanda Meyer
Maree and Randy Hougee

Maria Sultana
Marilyn Armato
Marlene Scicluna
Mary Catania
Megan Fromholtz, Lesley Williams and bubs
Michelle Briscoe
Natalie Allen-Howard
Nathan Hougee
Nicola Jackson
Rebecca Cauchi
Renee Caruana
Sanna Nilsson
Shelley and David Skogstad
Tamara Baird
Tyrone Pistofian